ONE MAN'S CHRISTMAS

ONE MAN'S CHRISTMAS

LEON HALE

Winedale Publishing

Houston

New and revised edition, September, 2015
Published by Winedale Publishing
3711 San Felipe, 6-B, Houston, TX 77027
Website address: www.winedalepublishing.com

Original edition, 1984, Shearer Publishing
Copyright © 1984, 2015 Leon Hale

ISBN 978-1-62349-384-4

Illustrated by Ken Muenzenmayer
Book design by David Timmons

Manufactured in the United States of America

For Mark, Becky, Daniel, Kacy and Travis

Contents

The Santa Claus Auxiliary

Early in the 1950s when my children were little, I was a member of a group called the Santa Claus Auxiliary. The only time we met was late on Christmas Eve. We met in the street, in kitchens, driveways, garages, living rooms, back-yards. Sometimes the meetings wouldn't break up until 1 or 2 a.m.

The purpose of our organization was to help Santa Claus. Along about that time he was having distribution problems. Our block was a fair example of why the trouble existed.

To start with, it was a very big block. It had thirty houses. Every house was the same size. Every one was built in 1950. Every one cost $11,500, had a combination GI-FHA loan, and a monthly mortgage payment of $74. Every family had 2.8 children averaging four years of age. Every breadwinner made almost the same amount of money. And Santa Claus left just about the same kind and number of presents at every house.

This was during the Baby Boom and all across the country, on blocks similar to ours, population was increasing at an extraordinary rate. You see, then, why Santa Claus was having trouble. There hasn't been a time, before or since, that so many little children over the world went to bed expecting that Santa would visit them before the sun came up on Christmas morning.

The result was, the old boy couldn't make his deliveries without help. He wasn't prepared. The footballs and basketballs he'd leave wouldn't be inflated. Sometimes the dolls wouldn't have a stitch of clothes on. The toy filling stations in their cardboard boxes wouldn't be assembled.

We organized the auxiliary to give Santa a little help. We did have a part in creating the problem so we felt an obligation to assist in its solution.

Organizing the auxiliary came about gradually. In the beginning, you would go outside at midnight after the children finally got to sleep and you would meet this worried-looking fellow carrying a flat basketball. He would want to know if you had a bicycle pump.

So you joined up with him and went round knocking on doors, asking for bicycle pumps. That was a rule. You had to help a guy find a bicycle pump to inflate a basketball and then in return he'd help you find a three-sixteenths-inch nut lost off the wheel bolt of a brand new scooter.

After a couple of Christmases a few specialists emerged. Down toward the east end of the block, there was a guy who became a respected tricycle mechanic. If you never have helped Santa Claus get presents ready for children, you might think there's no way a new tricycle would need any repair work done on it at one o'clock Christmas morning. Well, you'd be wrong.

Listen, one time a little after midnight on Christmas I went outside and saw a 33-year old father weaving down the middle of our street, riding a new tricycle. He was steering with one hand and singing "Jingle Bells." In his other hand he held a highball glass. Celebrating, yes. Celebrating not just the holiday but also the fact that, at last, his 2.8 kids had fallen asleep and the presents had been delivered.

A gent doing that is apt to break a pedal off a new trike. When that happened, it was sure a tragedy. Earthquakes weren't as serious.

So what you did, you steered that fellow down to the tricycle mechanic, who was a quiet, grinning Catholic and the father of five youngsters. If it hadn't been for him and his wife, and three or four free-wheeling protestant couples, our block would have had only 2.1 children per family.

He had a workshop in his garage. He had tools that plugged in and hummed. He was a hero. He saved marriages. He knew about such mysteries as left-hand threads on tricycle pedals. He had bolts and nuts and clamps and screws and

he could fix anything in the middle of the night.

With leadership like that, our little group was able to carry out planned projects, and not just emergency repair. One time we erected a basket-ball goal in total darkness, and almost without the use of swear words. I was proud that my personal post-hole diggers made the excavation.

Living on that block taught me that a man can earn respect in a neighborhood by owning post-hole diggers. Even the tricycle mechanic didn't own such a tool. My diggers weren't used very often, but all the holes they dug were important holes.

The charter members of the Auxiliary moved off that block, to places we thought were better. They weren't, though, not really. Sometimes I go back to the street and drive along it and feel proud. Good people moved in behind us. The block looks better than it ever did. The trees we planted—some of them in holes made by my diggers—are grown up and shading the street, and the houses are kept painted and maintained and that's good.

I've been thinking several years now I'd like to go back on a Christmas Eve, about midnight, and see if I could spot a young father going from house to house, looking for a bicycle pump.

Pure Magic

Sometimes you hear little children worrying, a few days ahead of Christmas, that Santa Claus won't be able to get in the house by way of the chimney. You see them peering up the flue, measuring that small opening against the size of the Santa Claus they saw in the department store and it's clear there's not enough room.

Other youngsters fret because their houses don't have chimneys at all, and the doors are locked at night, so how is Santa going to get in?

When they ask their mamas and papas about

this, the parents generally say, "Don't worry about it." What sort of answer is that? Little children deserve a better one, based on reason.

The facts are not recorded but in books you can find hints and clues and evidence enabling anybody with half a cup of brains to figure out the only possible answer. Which is, that in all ways Santa Claus is a magic person.

It doesn't make any difference to him how small an opening a chimney has. He can still come down it. If he needs to he can come down a stovepipe. He can come down it even if the damper is shut.

He can walk through doors, open or closed, locked or not. He can change his shape and appearance and be in forty places at once and maybe more.

For a foundation to support these conclusions, we can turn to the first person ever to see Santa Claus enter a house. This was one Clement C. Moore. He not only saw Santa come down a chimney but go back up it as well, on the night of December 24, 1821, in the city of New York.

Moore wrote an eye-witness account of this sighting and it turned out to be a pretty good poem, *A Visit From Saint Nicholas*, the one that begins, "'Twas the night before Christmas, when all through the house. . ."

In this account, Moore writes that he was about to go to sleep when heard a racket. He flung open a window and saw a *miniature* sleigh, eight *tiny* reindeer, and a *little* old driver.

Pay attention to those adjectives. Miniature. Tiny, Little.

Consider the sleigh. Do you imagine that a person who isn't magic could carry in a miniature sleigh enough presents for every house on the planet? No way. The sleigh wouldn't have anywhere near enough capacity.

Then the reindeer. Moore said Santa Claus yelled at the tiny deer and they flew to the top of the house. To begin with, your ordinary reindeer is not tiny. He's pretty good sized. In the second place, he can't fly. He can run and paw and prance and jump some, and that's about his limit.

I challenge you, then, to conclude anything

except that Santa Claus can change the size of sleighs and reindeer just when he feels the need of it. He can make a sleigh as big as a depot or he can shrink it down to where you could stick it in your vest pocket. It's hard to believe but the evidence is there. What trouble would it be for a person to change the size of a sleigh if he can make an animal fly when it hasn't even got wings?

It's clear enough, as well, that Santa can change the size of his own self.

When he appeared to Clement Moore that time, he was small. Moore referred to him as a *little* old driver. Said he had a droll *little* mouth. And a round *little* belly. Toward the end of his account, Moore called his visitor a right jolly old *elf*.

Elves are small, you know that. The Bureau of the Census says the average size of elves is a foot and half.

So how do you explain that when you go to a department store now and seen Santa, there he is six-foot-two and big around as a pickle barrel? The only explanation is: magic. He changes his size to fit the space he's got. He can also multiply himself and become hundreds of Santas all at once, and appear in stores across fifty states and several foreign countries and it isn't any strain on him.

If you're still not convinced, check the account of how Santa departed from Clement Moore's house. He put a finger alongside his nose, nodded, and *rose* up the chimney. Did Moore say Santa climbed up there? No. He didn't have to squat and leap, either. He didn't have to struggle or squeeze. He simply rose.

So don't worry. Anybody capable of magic like that isn't going to have trouble with chimney sizes. Or locked doors, either.

It Got Him Talking

Her name was Christina. She has been gone now for something like thirty years but at this season we often talk about Christina and her holiday parties.

Because at these gatherings she served fruit cake that tasted like no fruit cake you ever ate, and because her house was always decorated in ways that generated conversation.

We nibbled at her fruit cake and sipped the strange flavor of cider she served, and we talked about what Christina had done to her house this year.

She decorated with natural materials that weren't for sale anywhere. She'd go into the woods and gather branches with berries in various shades of red. She'd stalk across vacant lots, pulling up tall plants that you or I would call weeds. Around the middle of December we'd see her, in her flowing flowered skirt and her umbrella of a hat and we'd say, "There's Christina, gathering her Christmas stuff."

She never had a standard tree. The one I liked best, for a personal reason, was the dead pine. It was maybe eight feet tall and had been in a fire that took away all its greenery. She cleaned its limbs and brought that skeleton of a tree in the house. Trimmed it with curious ornaments made by Christina herself, or by poor little children she knew over in the ragged part of town.

If you asked her about the tree she'd say it pleased her to take a dead thing and make something pretty of it.

The main reason I liked going to Christina's

parties was that her house made me talk. At most parties I tend to sit silently in corners like a piece of antique furniture while everybody else carries on constant conversation. How can people think of so much to talk about?

In Christina's house there was always something odd in an interesting way. The pine tree, for instance. How could you look at a dead pine done up as a Christmas tree and not talk about it?

I found myself saying, out loud, to anybody who'd listen, that I was once married to an extraordinary lady, an artist, who decided one windy December day that she wanted a tumbleweed for a Christmas tree.

A couple of days later she announced she had found a truck driver who was loaded and headed out for a West Texas town called Matador, and on his return trip he would bring her a tumbleweed.

I had my doubts about that plan. Oh, I didn't doubt that she'd gone to a truck stop and located a driver going in the right direction. And I could see him grinning, and hear him saying sure, sure, he'd be glad to bring her a tumbleweed. Because that woman was powerfully persuasive. I just didn't believe he would really do it.

Then about a week before Christmas an 18-wheeler pulled up in front of the house and a truck driver came down from the cab and delivered a large tumbleweed. I have to tell you that I didn't see this happen, since I was on the road at the time. But that's the story I got and I hope it's right because I love being able to call up that scene, of a West Texas tumbleweed being delivered in Houston by one of those big highway rigs.

When decorated, the weed made a nice Christmas tree.

At Christina's party I told that story, with very few ornaments attached, and it was pretty well received. I was encouraged. So I told another one, about letting my kids do all the Christmas decorating that time.

They were twelve and ten, give or take a year, and we took a family vote and decided that this year the children would be privileged to do the holiday decoration. Buy the tree. Trim it. Everything. They were thrilled.

We lived then just behind a large shopping center. (Not recommended as an ideal environment for child rearing.) I gave them money and off they went, and stayed gone a long time. Finally returned with armloads of stuff.

Their main purchase was a large artificial Christmas tree. Came in a box half the size of a coffin. Its branches sprouted silvery plastic foliage. Each needed to be fitted into holes in the tree's trunk, a tedious job. Before it was done they said I could help if I wanted to but I said no, I wanted them to enjoy what they purchased.

They also bought an electric color wheel, designed to sit on the floor and throw its beams of color into the tree's silvery foliage. These interior decorators chose to perch the wheel up on the container it came in, so when an observer looked into our picture window he saw not just the tree but the color wheel sitting on a cardboard box.

I did point out that this spoiled the effect but the decorators said no, they wanted the public to see the wheel that produced all those colors because it cost almost as much as the tree.

Figaro the family cat agreed, fell in love with the box and took up residence inside it. Sometimes he knocked the wheel off onto the floor, and for long periods observers were treated to a display of Northern Lights flashing across the ceiling of our living room.

The great Christmas purchase included several canisters of fake snow. You know the kind. Shake it up and hit the button and out comes this white flaky stuff that you can use to create vast visual pollution. Our decorators squirted that gunk on all our windows that faced the street.

So that window glass became a snowy mural, with skies crowded by crude winged creatures I thought were wounded birds. But no, come on, they were angels. They stayed with us long past the holidays.

They resisted all attempts to wipe them off the glass. Years later when that house was sold, on our picture window you could still see the vague image of those angels.

The Christmas Eve Rush

The night before Christmas, a few minutes before the drugstore closed, I ran into my friend Mel back near the prescription counter. He was picking over a long table of toys that had been marked down thirty percent.

He made a little confession to me. Said his grandchildren were spending Christmas with him and he was afraid what he had bought them wasn't quite enough. So at the last hour he had sneaked out to spend a few more dollars and try to make certain their presents would be adequate.

I watched while he selected two stuffed animals that cost almost ten bucks apiece, even with the discount. My guess was his grandkids would take one look at those fake animals and pitch them under the bed.

But I understand why Mel bought those late gifts. They weren't really for his grandchildren. They were for him, so he could sleep better. He was suffering from Depression Christmas Syndrome, a disease that's common to guys our age.

He remembers a lot of Christmases when nobody got what they wanted in the way of presents, and what they did get was mighty slim. He remembers the pain of it, the disappointment. And he can't stand for it to happen to people he loves.

I know this because I remember the same things, and I recognize the symptoms. They afflict people who were children in the hard times of the 1930s. People who are now grandparents. Keep an eye on them Christmas Eve. After the ten o'clock news, instead of going to bed the way they generally do, they'll be restless. Pretty soon

they'll say they're going up to the shopping center to get some ice cream, even though there are three cartons of ice cream in the freezer already. They've gone after late presents, so they can get rid of the gnawing notion that they haven't bought enough.

I'm pretty good at recognizing these symptoms because for a long time I had them myself. I used to go out on Christmas Eve and buy anything that was left in the store because I couldn't stand not to. In this way I acquired some real lemons in the way of gifts.

One time I bought a printing press. I had already spent more than my budget allowed but it wasn't enough to satisfy me. I would get to thinking that my kids would wake up Christmas morning and feel like I felt in 1930. That was the year I wanted a pocketknife and didn't get it, and this boy up the street named Carter something got a bicycle and I was outraged by the injustice of that.

So, recalling that feeling, thirty-five years later I attempted to dispel it by buying a printing press. I reasoned my offspring would like that, since their father worked for a newspaper and other print media. But it was a perfectly rotten press. It had rubber type and the roller wouldn't pick up ink right and I never did make it produce a line of legible type. I did try, and I'm the only one who did. The children never looked twice at the thing and by Easter I had given it to the garbage man, who didn't seem to think much of it either.

But that didn't cure me of rushing out and buying late gifts because every now and then, I would buy something good.

The hockey game, for example. I didn't even like it when I laid down twenty dollars that Christmas Eve and lugged the awkward thing home in the rainy darkness. I bought it because it was bulky, and would take up space under the tree.

Well, it was a wonderful toy. This was before game toys were all electronic. This one had levers and handles that you twisted and pushed to make the little metal players slap the hockey puck in the net. It was sturdy and it lasted. It could take punishment.

We had hockey tournaments with that rig. Grown neighbors came over and played with it and there was laughter and yelling and whistling and stomping. It was a furious game, and required skill and coordination and that was the best last-minute Christmas gift I ever bought.

The next-best was the rocket. I wish I could remember how the rocket was made, so I could reproduce it and put it back on the market. I think it would sell a million even today.

I bought it because it cost only a couple of bucks and that's about what I had left on me after all the other shopping was done. But I couldn't stand not to have one more little insurance policy against disappointment, so I got the rocket.

It was air-propelled. You pumped it up and hit the trigger and that little booger launched and I mean it went *up*, not just treetop high but maybe 120 feet. When it started down a little parachute with a metal man popped out and it floated down sometimes a block from where you shot it.

Man, we had us a time with that rocket. It was the best thing we got that year. It was the best thing anybody in the neighborhood got. We had big kids in the fifth and sixth grade, kids who got new motor scooters for Christmas, coming around and standing in line to shoot our rocket.

I am telling you all this so you'll know what they're up to when you see people sneaking around in the stores late on Christmas Eve, buying printing presses and stuffed animals that nobody wants. It's not that they've waited too long to shop. They're just trying to wipe away painful memories and sometimes they even buy the right gifts and it makes them feel a lot better.

Vittles

Back in those hard times that people of my generation enjoy talking about, there was an advantage to living in the country. The advantage was that there was plenty to eat out there. I can remember seeing bread-and-soup lines in the towns, where unfortunate folks would queue up to get free food from the government. But I can't recall the equivalent of a soup line in the country.

Except on special occasions like Christmas or Thanksgiving, country food didn't have much variety. On an ordinary day a family might get by on cornbread and black-eyed peas and molasses and milk. The next day they would have cornbread and black-eyed peas and molasses and milk. The next day, the same things again. But the pots were big and you could fill up.

I suspect the food wasn't anywhere near as good as I like to remember it, either. I base that suspicion on what we considered to be extra-special treats. An orange, for example.

If country food was so wonderful, why did we get excited about oranges? I don't remember ever eating an orange in the country except at Christmas. All the kids would get an orange apiece in their Christmas stockings and that was our citrus fruit for the year.

The brisk fragrance released when the skin of an orange was torn—that seemed so wonderful. It became for me the flavor of Christmas, of a special time. Even now when I put orange peels down the garbage grinder and hit the switch, the smell that comes up out of the sink makes me think of Christmas, no matter what time of year I do it.

So maybe it was the symbolism of the orange, rather than its goodness, that made it special in the country. But how about this: During spells of nostalgia, I've been guilty of describing with high enthusiasm the great cakes and pies the women would fix in those old country kitchens on wood-burning stoves. And yet, my favorite Christmas sweet to this day is chocolate-covered cherries out of the grocery store. When I first knew them they cost about thirty-five cents a box, for two layers of those juicy sweethearts. I felt that a four-layer Christmas cake made by my favorite grandmother wasn't anything but minor league, for taste, against chocolate-covered cherries.

I have struggled against this notion, and lost. So I have quit talking about it to people it offends. At Christmas I sneak away to the supermarket and buy a box of cherries and hide it in the back of the refrigerator. I save every cherry for myself. I eat the entire box. They cost a lot more than thirty-five cents now.

Among the holiday desserts those women made in their wood-burning stoves, my favorite is sweet potato pie. If that has the sound of Hard Times, let it be. I always liked the rhythm in the name. Sweet potato pie. I found a comfort in it.

The reason was, we always had what it takes to make this fine pie. We had lard and flour for the crust and we sure had the sweet potatoes. Man, did we ever. Dogs under the house didn't have fleas the way we had sweet potatoes. And if we were short of sugar, there was always molasses as a substitute. I think molasses makes a better pie anyhow.

At the end of this story you will find a nice recipe for sweet potato pie, made with lard crust. Most people will want to put in the sugar but if you have really good yams with a high sugar content, the potatoes and the molasses produce plenty of sweetness. At least for me they do. I like a sort of spare taste in this pie. It's a Hard Times pie and ought not to be excessive. Which may sound hollow, coming from a dude who also wants the sweet syrupiness of chocolate-covered cherries, but never mind that.

Something else I remember about holiday

meals in the country is the con game that adults
worked on the children, about what was good to
eat. A turkey drumstick, for instance. The small-
est children always yelled for a drumstick off a
Christmas turkey and the adults were willing to
let them have it, seeing the thing was practically
inedible.

At a Texas Christmas table today, the children
are likely to be served first and get the choice bits
of everything. In my early times, adults took the
opposite course. That was before we entered the
child-worship era. The children were served last

and often by themselves, where they couldn't see that their parents were getting all the best parts of the bird.

No mature person cared anything about eating the leg off a 1932-model turkey tom. Because that bird's leg was mostly all bone and gristle. He grew up in pastures, chasing grasshoppers and lizards and running in desperation from coyotes. That turkey was in *shape*. Nothing about his leg was tender.

But the adults would say, "Man, ain't nothin' like a drumstick." True enough, if you don't count table legs.

I spent several Christmas dinners gnawing at a turkey drumstick before I caught the grown-ups grinning at me, between their bites of white meat slathered in giblet gravy.

If you try the sweet potato pie, I wish you'd make at least two of them. Put the sugar in one, and use only the molasses in the other, and see which one you like better. Let me know.

Sweet Potato Pie

1 lb. sweet potatoes

1 tbs. butter

2 eggs

½ cup milk

½ cup sugar

2 tbs. unsulphured molasses

1 tbs. bourbon whiskey (or vanilla extract)

⅛ tsp. salt

¼ tsp. cinnamon (plus 2 extra shakes)

¼ tsp. nutmeg (plus 2 extra shakes)

¼ tsp. all-spice (plus 2 extra shakes)

A 9- or 10-inch uncooked pie crust, made
    with lard

Boil potatoes in the skins until tender. While potatoes are still warm, skin them and mash thoroughly with the butter in a large mixing bowl. In another bowl, beat the eggs, milk and sugar together with an egg beater or electric mixer. Add

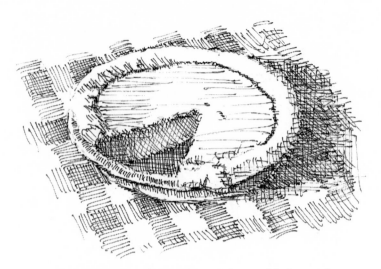

this mixture to the potatoes, then add the molasses, whiskey, salt and spices.

Beat the pie filling until it is very smooth. Now taste it. If it tastes a little *too* sweet, that's good, because a lot of the sweetness cooks out of it in the oven. If it doesn't taste sweet enough to you, add a little sugar, but not too much.

Pour the filling into the crust and bake in a 400° oven until the center puffs up and a toothpick inserted near the middle comes out clean (about 40-45 minutes).

Christmas Poker

In the Brazos River Bottom I've got an old friend who is a retired fortuneteller. In her earlier times she worked for various small carnivals and traveled about the country and lived a curious life. She calls herself Madame Z, which is her carnival name.

A few days before Christmas I always drive into the Bottom and take Madame a gift. This time I had brought her an item of costume jewelry in the shape of a great beetle, dipped in gold paint and sporting six striped legs.

Madame has a weakness for such paste, and it had put her into a storytelling mood, which is what I always hope anytime I go into the Bottom to see her. She was in the big rocking chair there in her shack and wearing one of her flashier rigs—the navy dress with the orange flowers.

"I suppose the best Christmas I ever had," she said, "was in '34 in East Saint Looie. Did I ever tell you about that?"

"That was the year I was working for Major Sabinas, a Spanish fellow out of Nogales who was running a little carny. Christmas is generally a lonesome time for carnies because it's the season for homes, and families. Carnies don't have homes except what they find on the road, and they never have families at all.

"The weather had caught us at East Saint Looie—well, wait. Maybe it was Quincy, or Granite City. Anyway it was there along the Mississippi, one side or the other. It had a domino hall called Poor Frank's. This was about dark on Christmas Eve, and the Major and myself and

Cuffs Wilson were sitting in Poor Frank's, mainly waiting on time.

"Cuffs Wilson was one of the Major's drivers. He was called Cuffs because he bought shirts six inches too long at the sleeves, and turned them back several times so that when he played cards he could hide useful objects in the folds. Such as an extra ace.

"Anyway, the door to Poor Frank's opened that night and in came this little sad-eyed gent, all meek and wrinkled, and said he was from the Lost Hope Orphanage over by the river. He said the Lost Hope was where twenty-two little kids lived, and they had no Christmas tree, and no presents, and not much to eat, and furthermore they had no mamas or papas. So it sounded like he was clouding up to put the touch on us. The Major was about to give him the heave but then the little gent stated his game.

"He said he had a five-spot on him, which was the last cent in the till at the Lost Hope Orphanage, and he was looking for a card game in hopes of increasing his roll so he could buy Christmas for the little kids.

"This interested the Major, and Cuffs as well, since they were the sort who would take a five-spot off their grandmother, if she wasn't armed. So they sat the Major down and relieved him of the five bucks in one hand of draw power. He got up, slow and droopy, with tears on his wrinkled cheeks, and went out into the night.

"The Major laughed, and said anybody who would bet two jacks into a one-card draw deserved to be cleaned out. And Cuffs Wilson said the sad-eyed gent was the weakest mullet he had come across on the tour.

"Well, I got up then and left Poor Frank's and I wasn't feeling real well. I walked around a long time, and my insides got to gnawing at me about those little orphan kids. So I bought a couple of turkeys, and candy, and fruit, and other stuff little kids like at Christmas, and lugged it over to the Lost Hope Orphanage.

"On the front porch I peeked in and saw this peculiar sight. There in the living room was the

Major himself, standing on a stepladder and putting a star on a Christmas tree about twelve feet tall, and surrounding him were twenty-two little orphan kids. Then there was this loud ho-ho-ho from down the hall, and in came a Santa Claus all loaded with dolls, and footballs, and scooters, and every kind of present small orphan kids might want. And right away I saw the Santa Claus wasn't anybody but Cuffs Wilson because his shirt cuffs were sticking six inches out of the sleeves of his red suit.

"Well, I went on in, and delivered my goods, and watched while Cuffs handed out the loot, and we had a big supper, and sang carols, and the little sad-eyed gent stood back in a corner the whole time, and I could see tears slipping down his wrinkles.

"It was maybe midnight when we got back to Poor Frank's Place. That was the best Christmas I ever had, like I say. It wasn't even spoiled when Poor Frank explained to us that the little sad-eyed gent came into his place every Christmas

Eve, and invested a five-spot in a card game just that same way. And it never failed to get Christmas delivered to the orphanage."

A Five-footer With a Bad Side

Exactly what year it was I can't say. But I won't forget that I was living then in the dog house, just four days before Christmas.

The source of this disfavor was my announcement that I needed to go see my parents.

Right now? With the house decorated and the tree trimmed? And company coming the day after tomorrow? And the children all excited about Christmas? And I wanted to leave, and drive three hundred miles to visit my mother and father?

Yes, but don't worry, I'd make it a flying trip. Get up early when the traffic was light. Be there by mid-afternoon. Spend only one night. Get back home before dark on Thursday.

But why?

Well, it was just something I needed to do. My folks were growing old. My father was recovering from a heart attack, and not doing so well. Something in the tone of my mother's voice, on the phone, had told me I needed to go.

So I went.

And when I arrived I was shocked by the atmosphere in their house. The very air in those rooms seemed heavy, and troubled. In normal times this was a busy, talkative couple but I found them subdued, almost silent.

They said Oh, don't worry, they'd be OK. It was simply that lately a lot of things hadn't been going right. There'd been trouble with the car. My mother's old cat had run off, and hadn't come back yet. My father's little bedside radio had gone on the blink, and you know how he is about that radio. A good neighbor across the street had died. Things like that.

They hadn't put up a tree. Didn't they intend to have a Christmas tree?

No, they'd decided to forget about Christmas this year. With only the two of them there, fixing up for the holidays didn't seem worth the trouble.

That evening my father talked about how he might never be able to return to work, and he wasn't ready to retire. My mother made a pie to take across the street to the neighbor, and she was unhappy with it. Seemed like nothing she cooked lately turned out right. Before she went to bed she stood at the back door, one more time, and called the cat. That cat had disappeared before, but had never stayed gone this long.

The next morning early I had my overnight bag zipped up and was ready to go home when I made my little speech. About how I hated to leave, so close to Christmas when they weren't feeling well.

They said No, you go on, back to your wife and kids where you belong.

Maybe those last three words made it clear to me where I really belonged, on that day.

I dropped my bag and said I'd return in half an hour. Drove away and found a fellow selling Christmas trees on a vacant lot. He didn't have many left but I got a five-footer with a bad side. Back at the house I discovered some pine boards in the garage and built a sort of stand. I put the bad side of the tree to the wall and it looked all right.

From the hall closet I got down two sturdy cardboard boxes the family had used to store Christmas decorations since the time of my awareness. There were lights, but they were the old kind, wired so that one burned-out bulb would turn off every light on the string. And you could spend half an hour screwing in and taking out bulbs, looking for the bad one.

So I was sitting on the living room rug doing the bad-bulb routine and I glanced up at my father, in what he always called his easy chair. He was smiling at my struggles. The only smile I'd seen in the house since I arrived.

I gave up on the old lights and went to the drugstore for new ones. Before I left I grabbed the little radio and took it to a shop I remembered, near the department store where my father worked. I asked the shop man if he could fix the radio, quick, like right now. He looked at it and said no, but he could sell me a new one at a good price, and he did.

Decorating a Christmas tree without assistance was a new experience for me and the result wasn't beautiful. In the cardboard boxes my mother had even saved icicles, those thin strips of foil you draped over branches of the tree. A tedious procedure, and I was never any good at it.

My mother wanted to help but by this time I'd become stubborn about doing everything myself. She sat on the edge of a chair, her back straight, hands folded, not quite comfortable about work going on under her roof when she wasn't involved in it.

In the bottom of one of the boxes I came across an ornament made by one of my sisters when she was maybe eight years old—a fat Santa

Claus, scissored out of red construction paper, his fading beard drawn on with a white Crayola. The figure was about to fall apart and hadn't been used in years. But I knew it was an ornament my mother valued above all the world's fancy store-bought Christmas glitz.

So I put it on the very top of the tree, where an angel usually goes, or a star. It sat up there a little crooked but I could tell my mother approved.

Next I went back out and ranged around and bought presents. Cheap ones, but quite a few. I was looking mainly for volume. Some were joke gifts, like the necktie. My father was a dresser, and loved nice ties. In a variety store I found this loud job with red-white-and-blue stripes and it made me grin so I bought it.

Before I quit I agonized a while about what to get for my mother. The best thing, of course, would be the cat. Man, if I could find that cat.

But that was just Christmas wishing. I couldn't find a lost cat. Wouldn't be any point in looking. And yet I did, sort of, long enough to see that, tonight at least, dogs had the upper hand.

Back at the house I sneaked all my loot into a bedroom and shut the door and wrapped every gift. If anybody ever sponsors a contest for bad gift wrapping, put your money on me. When I get through with them, my gifts look like they've been through a car wash. But when I piled them beneath the tree, they generated impressive remarks, like Good Grief, Great Scot, and Lord Have Mercy.

Along about dark I plugged in the tree and turned down the lights in the living room, and I said OK folks, gather round, Santa Claus has come, and we're gonna have Christmas.

My plan was that we could sing together, maybe *Silent Night*, before we opened gifts. We used to do that when I was a kid. We were a singing bunch. But I cancelled the singing because I decided I'd never get past mother and child without bawling like a hungry baby. I was trying to lift spirits, not generate tears.

I'd love to tell you that playing Santa Claus for my parents was a great success, which was not the case. But it wasn't a failure, either. They went along with it, and said all the right things, and smiled a lot.

Next morning when I went out to the car to leave, they both walked out with me, and they were talking, and laughing about the presents. My father was wearing his robe, and he had the red-white-and-blue necktie draped across his shoulders.

I got home twenty-four hours late so I was still in the dog house. But I've always been glad I took that flying Santa Claus trip because what I didn't know—what none of us knew then—was that my mother already had a cancer that would soon kill her, and I would never again see both my parents together at Christmas.

Miracles Out of a '22 Chevy

The best Christmas I remember out of my early times was in 1930. I spent it on a wind-scalded sheep ranch about forty miles southwest of Fort Worth, near Granbury. I hated that ranch but a special thing happened there that Christmas.

All that fall my father was off working somewhere and my mother was staying on the ranch, cooking and taking care of two little girls whose own mother was sick and dying in Fort Worth. In those times we moved around a lot to perform unhappy duties that had to be carried out. Things were not good. One of my sisters and I didn't even go to school that winter. We existed, out in that lonely place.

When I read now about a dwelling that's hard and pitiless, I visualize the little thin-walled house we stayed in and I think of emptiness.

A square-built house. Four rooms counting the kitchen. A cistern in the backyard. A wash bench with tubs. A clothesline strung from the corner of the house to the back gatepost. The yard was enclosed by a sheep fence but there was no grass that needed protection from sheep. No flowers. Not one shrub to soften things. The yard was hard gray clay, studded with chalky rocks and scoured by dust.

The house was on top of a broad mound. Not so much a hill but more a great bulge in the earth's skin, a quarter of a mile in diameter. It's the nature of men that they look for high places to build homes. I expect the person who built that house would say he put it on the rise to catch the breeze in summer, to cool the bedroom and drive the windmill. But in winter when the northers came, the top of that barren rise was cold without mercy. A slashing, demoralizing cold that withered the spirit.

The wind almost never rested. There was always its swish and bluster in the ears, and the flapping and popping of clothes on the line. Clothes my mother scrubbed so many times they were worn more from washing than from wearing.

The highway into Granbury was five hundred yards to the south of the front door. To the east, west, and north, no trees for half a mile. Then finally there were thin stands of mesquite and scrub oak, their branches tortured by wind and drouth.

On high-windy afternoons the sky often got yellow with dust. My sister and I would take the babies down in the pasture to be among trees, to find relief from the harsh light and the noise of the wind and the popping of the clothes on the line.

Also, to give my mother time alone so she could pray. That's what she did when we left her

alone. I sometimes spied on her, I confess. When she thought we were off in the mesquite she would stand in front of the wood cookstove and shut her eyes and raise her face to the ceiling and pray desperately. It filled me with a dreadful sadness for her to pray that way. Things must have been mighty bad, if they needed to be prayed over

that hard and that often. To this day most prayers are sad to me, full of anxiety and pleading.

That ranch had no barn. I never forgave it that shortcoming. We had been on farms before in our moving about and they always had barns. Sometimes they were big friendly barns with grain bins and hay lofts and horse stalls and ladders and a thousand secret places to explore and to feel warm and safe in, even when alone.

But the ranch had, other than the little house, only a woodpile and a set of pens and a low-slung shed, a combination feed and tack room so full you couldn't even go inside it.

No men were on that place, not in the sense that men live and work on ranches. My father was a traveling salesman much of his life and I was accustomed to his not being home, but that December of 1930, I missed him in a desperate way. The only man we ever saw was my uncle, the father of the two little children my mother cared for. His wife was the one who was sick. He managed that little ranch but not for money, only for the use of the house.

Few sheep were left on the place then and my uncle worked in Granbury and ran back and forth a lot to Fort Worth. Sometimes we wouldn't see him for ten days running because he'd come home late and leave long before we woke up.

I admired that man fiercely, and wanted to be like him, to look like him. He was a genuine cow man. A roper and a rider and a bronc buster and he knew about ranching. You know what kind of work he did, to feed those babies and pay for his wife's care? He washed dishes in a dingy cafe in Granbury.

A dishwasher! This proud man, who ought to have been riding a fine horse through a herd of good cattle, doing what he was meant and fitted for, and here he was a dishwasher.

When the weather began to get cold sometimes he would come home during the day for a couple of hours and walk to the timber and cut firewood. I would follow him, and watch. I would keep back, though, because he didn't want to talk. He worked with astonishing speed, almost with violence. It was if the trunk of a mesquite represented his burden and he tried to cut it away with the ax.

Once I saw him drop the ax, sink to the ground, and sob. Even then I understood why, though I couldn't have gotten it into words. He simply had to cry away some of the weight that was on him. Otherwise it would have been too much, and he couldn't have kept on. That wife of his couldn't have been much past thirty, and she wasn't going to get well, and the dishwashing job wasn't near covering expenses. December had come, and his two little girls in that dreary house were already talking about Christmas. It was too big a load, without sitting by a mesquite stump and crying a part of it off.

I had a little burden of my own along about then. I had the gnawing feeling that my father had gone off and deserted us. I never mentioned it. I was afraid to ask because I didn't want to hear that it was true. Maybe he was off washing some dishes of his own, doing whatever anybody would pay him for, the way so many men did in those strange times. But nobody talked about where he was, or what he might be doing.

One thing was clear to us all in that house, there wouldn't be any Christmas. So as December wore along you could almost feel the sinking of spirits on that lonely hill.

Then suddenly one day they said he was coming. To me it was like he was returning from the

dead. I can hear him now, coming, chugging up that road in his 1922-model Chevy. I can still get the first glimpse of that shivering old car when it came curving out of the timber. I can see the steam trailing out of the radiator cap. I'm running to the road and he's turning in and I can see the gray boot showing through the hole in the left front tire. I can see the twist in the wire that holds the door shut on the driver's side. He's waiting for me to open the gate and I can see him grinning and his eyes are all wet and his Adam's apple is bobbing in his long neck and his skinny arm is out the window and hanging there curved, waiting to grab me.

That's the day I discovered you can cry about happy things, that tears can rise out of gladness, and they can be hard to stop.

Miracles. That man brought miracles to a place of sadness. By supper we were singing and dancing. The next morning we went across the road and cut a skimpy little cedar and built a stand for it. We popped the popcorn he brought and strung it for decoration. We cut strips of colored paper out of a mail-order catalog and made Christmas chains held together with flour-and-water paste. We looped cranberries on lengths of thread. And all of these things we put on the tree.

We cut out a cardboard star and covered it with tinfoil, and we topped off the cedar with that star and thought the pitiful thing was pretty.

Then on the Day, more miracles. An air rifle! It was forty times more than I dreamed I'd get. And he brought a doll and a coat for my sister. A dress and some beads for my mother and she actually laughed when she opened the package.

There were more dolls for the little girls and a new cowboy shirt for my uncle, and it fit, and made him smile. I wonder how long it had been since that poor man smiled.

That wasn't all. He brought a turkey, fruits, nuts, candy, bakery bread already sliced. I thought, well, he's robbed a store somewhere, because how else could a person acquire such wealth without breaking the law? I never did ask. We talked about that Christmas a hundred times across the years, but I never did ask him where he got all that stuff.

The greatest gift he came with, he had funny stories to tell, and happy songs for us to sing while he played his harmonica. There was a moment during all this that an astonishing thought went loping across my mind. I looked at the walls of that little house, at the cedar that sagged to the left, and the Christmas star that had warped, and I thought, "This is a beautiful place."

CPSIA information can be obtained
at www.ICGtesting.com
Printed in the USA
LVOW12s0311220916
505489LV00002BA/2/P